Celebrating Children's 12 Genius Qualities

Kathy Koch, Ph.D.,
Tina Hollenbeck, and
Brad Sargent

CELEBRATE KIDS, INC.
FORT WORTH, TX

Kathy Koch, Ph.D./Celebrate Kids, Inc.
P.O. Box 136234,
Fort Worth, TX, 76136
admin@celebratekids.com,
www.celebratekids.com

Book Layout Nancy Matheis ©2013 BookDesignTemplates.com

Ordering Information:
Special discounts are available on quantity purchases by schools,
associations, and others. For details, contact admin at the above
address.

Celebrating Children's 12 Genius Qualities
Kathy Koch, Ph.D., Tina Hollenbeck, and Brad Sargent —1st ed.
ISBN 978-1-941062-07-4

Printed in the United States of America

Contents

To all the moms and dads who know their child is a genius.

[1]

Multiple Intelligences

Whether this is your first connection with Celebrate Kids, Inc., or you've been introduced to our work already, we're glad you're here – and welcome! Our purpose is to inspire, encourage, and equip you to become better as a parent, educator, and/or mentor to the children and teenagers in your life. To help you influence the kids you're connected with, we've produced materials on a variety of relevant topics, including people's core needs, learning styles, and personal growth.

This particular booklet focuses on the 12 Genius Qualities that we believe every person has as potentials which they can develop. This material arises from our interaction with the theory and application of Multiple Intelligences and, more specifically, with the related research on genius qualities by educator Dr. Thomas Armstrong. But, if we're going to learn about awakening and keeping genius qualities alive, we'll need to know what each of those terms mean.

Dr. Thomas Armstrong notes in his book, **Awakening Genius in the Classroom**:

> [T]he word *genius* ... has come to be associated with elite performances: scores of 130 or higher on I.Q. tests; extraordinary feats in music, art, and literature; and the very highest demonstrations of human competence in other domains as well. (page v)

"Extra high intelligence," "genius," and "creative" giftedness have all become fused in our perception as a society. But what does this do for and to the "average" person – if there actually is such a creature? Can the "everyday" man or woman, girl or boy, express genius qualities even if they don't have superhero intelligence or "mad skills" for creative arts or inventing?

We agree with Dr. Armstrong and say a hearty, "Yes!" We're convinced these are actual, innate qualities, not just theoretical concepts, and that they really do apply to every child, everywhere, and not just to some mysteriously elevated individuals.

Dr. Kathy and Tina will write about each of the 12 Genius Qualities that Dr. Armstrong identified. But first, let's pull up to our mental microscope for a moment to examine essential facts from the two concepts of intelligence and genius. This provides the background we need for when we switch over to our imagination telescopes, and explore new horizons among the stars.

"Intelligence" and "Multiple Intelligences"

At one time, *intelligence* was all about performance on the I.Q. test. Results on this test mapped out to a standard bell curve, with an I.Q. of 100 points being the exact middle of the curve – the average. Then, an equal number of test-takers received scores lower than 100 as received higher than 100. Also, the distribution of scores on each side of the midline declines symmetrically – the farther you go from the midline, the fewer people there are who hold that score.

In this system, I.Q. test scores of 130 or more are generally considered to be at the level of *genius*, as noted in the quote from Dr. Armstrong. This score represents the 98th percentile (top 2%) of test-takers. It is also the minimum equivalent for joining Mensa, which is probably the most well-known high-I.Q. society. A similar organization called One-in-a-Thousand Society (OATHS) is for those with I.Q. scores of at least 150; this represents just .1% of the population. (Yes, the decimal point is not a misprint. This is the 99.9th percentile – the top one-tenth of 1% of the I.Q. bell curve.)

Then along came developmental psychologist and educator Howard Gardner. His theory of **Multiple Intelligences** counteracts the notion that intelligence is simply the one be-all, end-all measure of overall intellectual capacity. His research presented in the groundbreaking **Frames of Mind: The Theory of Multiple Intelligences** (1983) suggested that linguistic and logical skills dominate the standardized I.Q. test. But there are so many other kinds of mental abilities that seem important. Why would only those two particular competences be relevant to creating a single-measure test of intellectual capacity? He theorized instead that:

- All people innately have the capacities for multiple kinds of intelligences.
- Each intelligence can be activated and grow, and if usage is stifled or stopped, it can be reactivated without losing all prior progress that had been made.
- People usually have about five or six of these intelligences well developed by the time they are adults. (When Dr. Gardner first released his theory, he identified seven of these multiple intelligences. He later added an eighth one – Naturalistic – and continued to research for more. For instance, he's suggested there is an Existential-Moral intelligence.)

So, the question is not, "How smart am I?" but "How am I smart?" At Celebrate Kids, Inc., we call these the "eight kinds of smart." We also use labels, first introduced by Dr. Thomas Armstrong when he worked with Dr. Gardner at Harvard University, which simplify Dr. Gardner's terms, to make it easier to communicate these concepts to kids.

Here are the two versions of those terms:

Dr. Howard Gardner	Celebrate Kids, Inc.
Linguistic	Word Smart
Logical-Mathematical	Logic Smart
Spatial	Picture Smart
Musical	Music Smart
Bodily-Kinesthetic	Body Smart
Naturalist	Nature Smart
Interpersonal	People Smart
Intrapersonal	Self Smart

The methodology behind all of this really is fascinating! Dr. Gardner used three key criteria for identifying an ability or capacity as one of the multiple intelligences:

1. He found people who lost a significant level of that ability, due to a stroke, brain injury, or other kind of **brain damage**.

2. He found people with a highly developed level of that same ability. *Savants* generally have only that ability at any significant level, and *prodigies* manifest high levels at a very early age.

3. He found individuals in history who are generally recognized as a *genius* in that ability.

So, it was significantly based in researching the case studies of real people. That is why his analysis yields rich and realistic descriptions of the qualities of those "smarts." You can find out more about Dr. Gardner's theory and how we apply this practically at Celebrate Kids, Inc., in Dr. Kathy's book, *8 Great Smarts Discover and Nurture You Child's Intelligences* (Moody Publishers, 2016) and other related items available on our website.

[2]

Genius Qualities

From Eight Multiple Intelligences to 12 Genius Qualities

If there has been one major concern about Multiple Intelligences by Dr. Gardner himself, it is that educators use these intelligences as individual add-ons instead of as an integrated organic system. In other words, they over-compartmentalize them and then work on each one too much individually – as if tinkering with a machine to improve its efficiency. Instead, they should see these intelligences as developing together as a whole for the betterment of one's humanity.

This concern has been echoed by Dr. Armstrong, who translated Dr. Gardner's technical material to be more accessible for the everyday reader in *7 Kinds of Smart: Identifying and*

Developing Your Multiple Intelligences (Plume, Revised Updated Edition, 1999). He sees them as needing to be integrated, not overly separated, and for the fulfillment of each person's greatest potential.

Dr. Armstrong is a big believer in people's potential. In fact, he was one of the first educators, way back in the 1970s, to change the phrase "learning disabled" to "learning different" when describing the children he worked with. He observed a brightness about them that encouraged him. He was very concerned about teaching and parenting methods and the use of medication to change children's behavior. In that light, he began asking, "Where have the geniuses gone?" By reading about Edison, Einstein, Bach, Franklin, Carver, and other "acknowledged adult geniuses," he identified 12 qualities they have in common. We'll be addressing them in the same order he first mentions them in his 1998 book, ***Awakening Genius in the Classroom***.

Dr. Armstrong used a similar case study analysis approach to that behind Multiple Intelligences, only he took a deeper look at people we consider geniuses and what exactly makes them "tick." Part of what drove him was a desire "toward honoring the different kinds of knowing that exist in our students" (page viii). He was also concerned about the greater emphasis among educators on ***disabilities*** in learners than on their

abilities. He sought to restore some of the dance and romance that leads to joyful learning and application.

Dr. Armstrong notes that these qualities "are supported ... by research in the neurosciences, anthropology, developmental psychology, and other sources" (page 3) including biographical studies. He identified people throughout history who are commonly seen as creative geniuses and inventors, and others with extraordinary stories of learning. He studied their lives and extracted his 12 Genius Qualities from similarities in their stories. His book mentions:

- Scientists like Thomas Edison, Albert Einstein, and Sir Alexander Fleming.
- Artists Pablo Picasso and Henri Matisse.
- Writers Shakespeare and Dr. Samuel Johnson.
- Composer Johann Sebastian Bach.
- Inventors George Washington Carver and Benjamin Franklin.
- Advocate and activist Helen Keller.
- Modern dancer Martha Graham.

Here's the list of common qualities he developed:
1. Curiosity
2. Playfulness
3. Imagination
4. Creativity

5. Wonder
6. Wisdom
7. Inventiveness
8. Vitality
9. Sensitivity
10. Flexibility
11. Humor
12. Joy

In the same spirit as Multiple Intelligences, Dr. Armstrong theorizes that:

- All people are innately open to these genius qualities related to the sheer joy of learning, even if they do not fit the conventional definition (or stereotype) of being "a genius" in the 99th percentile on standardized I.Q. tests, (page 1) or artistically "gifted."
- Each capacity or quality can be awakened and grow.
- If development of a quality is stifled or stopped, it can be reactivated without losing all prior progress that had been made.

Whether or not we develop any or all of these qualities is up to us. An additional choice we must consider then is whether we help those we influence to develop their genius.

"If multiple intelligences represent the rainbow of learning, then genius is the pot of gold at the end of the rainbow."

(page ix)

[3]

How the Genius Qualities Get Awakened

Using the word *genius* was deliberate and provocative, as Dr. Armstrong openly admits, just as was Dr. Gardner's purposeful use of plural *intelligences* to get people to think (page vi). By *genius*, Dr. Armstrong means **"giving birth to one's joy"** (page 1). This goes back to original meanings in the Greek and Latin word roots. He also says that "it is the genius of the student that is the driving force behind all learning" (page 2), and "a symbol for an individual's potential: all that a person may be that lies locked inside during the early years of development" (page 2).

Despite so many surrounding forces that would seek to shut genius qualities down, there are ways teachers – as well as young people's parents and mentors – can awaken these qualities in school and in life. Dr. Armstrong focuses on four principles:

- Reawaken the genius in yourself.
- Provide simple genius experiences while learning.
- Create a genial climate while learning.
- Know that genius is expressed in many ways.

Reawaken the Genius in Yourself

Our lives are tools that can help shape others. But sometimes it's difficult to keep in mind that we as role models need to demonstrate in behavior the ideas we want to convey. Dr. Armstrong reminds us that, "if you wish to spark the hidden light of genius that lives in every one of your students, you must first find and (re) light that spark in yourself" (page 49).

He challenges us to get through our disappointments and fears, and find inspiration instead of let ourselves stall in stagnation. One way to do this is to recall what used to draw our interest enough to find a state of creative "flow," and do something about them – not just be satisfied with dreams. Revive hobbies and activities that we've let fall into neglect. Play. Collect. Study or try something new. Rediscover what makes us feel truly alive! "the point is not to saddle yourself with a new list of things you have to do, read, or write for, but rather to allow yourself to be directed toward those activities that you want to do for their own sake" (page 55).

Provide Simple Genius Experiences

Here Dr. Armstrong emphasizes **simple** source materials and experiences, where children can combine, practice, move, observe, hear, question, manipulate, read, try, glue, taste, relate, etc. While presenting children with finished products can lead to inspiration, supplying raw materials instead leaves far more room for exploration and illumination – and the emotional surge of surprise, delight, and awe that can go with it.

Think of it as a version of show-and-tell to draw in children's interest in order to draw out their genius!

Create a Genial Climate

By genial, Dr. Armstrong emphasizes the overall energizing mood of the environments we create for learning and living. We need to be genial – moving in a mood of celebration that values the personhood and honors the potential of everyone around us. These are, of course, some of the core values for Celebrate Kids, Inc.! So, what is a genial learning environment? He notes five characteristics "that guide ... instruction regardless of content or grade level":

1. **Freedom to choose** from a variety of options for how to study, and how to express what they are learning.

2. **Open-ended exploration** where the routes, goals, and timing of the learning trajectory may be indefinite, unfixed, imprecise, unscripted, non-linear.

3. **Freedom from judgment** and from being dominated by systems built on ranking systems that promote some as elite and demote others as inferior. And when standardized tests are required, encourage kids that "their true mission is to focus on the intrinsic joy of learning" (page 63).

4. **Honoring of every student's experience**, regardless of how they compare with the experiences of adults or other kids. This helps create "an atmosphere of trust, mutual understanding, and diversity of opinion" (page 64).

5. **Belief in every student's genius**, and both acting and advocating consistently in accordance with that. This includes not negating in private what you state in public by downgrading or applauding the genius qualities of some. Dr. Armstrong shares a poignant quote from Goethe that if you "treat people as if they are what they ought to be, you help them to become what they are capable of being" (page 65).

It's also instructive to consider what constitutes the opposite of genial: "strictness, rigidity, boredom, criticism, or anxiety stifles the creative impulse and strangles any possibility for joy, humor, flexibility, or vitality" (page 60). Sadly, these kinds of environments stifle anyone's flow.

Know that Genius is Expressed in Many Ways

Just a very few individuals qualify as "a" genius by the conventional definition of a brilliant I.Q. but they have become our standard and measure for joyful learning, which includes these traits of "expressing" genius that we believe everyone starts out with. But how to bridge that gap?

Dr. Armstrong closes his short book by overviewing multiple intelligences. He believes it "comes closest to providing educators with a model that embraces a wide range of gifts in our students that are also represented in actual roles in the real world" (page 66). Yet even this system falls short of the unique profile of genius qualities every individual embodies. "this means that there are as many forms of genius in the classroom as there are students" (page 69).

It's difficult to retrain both the conscious and unconscious parts of ourselves to see expressions of genius as far more common than we've been conditioned to see. But we must change our paradigm if we hope to fulfill a motto we have here at Celebrate Kids, Inc.: "kids have present value, not just future potential."

Perhaps the word list on the next page will spark something awake in you, in considering how to activate the 12 genius qualities in yourself and those whom you've been given to influence. Most of these words will appear somewhere in the essays from Dr. Kathy and Tina that follow ... so watch for them!

Awakening Words

Activate	Encourage	Mature
Acknowledge	Engage	Notice
Active	Enliven	Openness
Allow	Enthuse	Pause
Antidote	Enthusiasm	Practice
Awakened	Excited	Praise
Begin	Exercise	Prepare
Bright	Expect	Pretend
Build	Experience	Prioritize
Celebrate	Experiment	Promote
Changes	Explore	Rabbit trials OK
Choose	Externalize	Redirect
Commit	Facilitate	Rediscover
Compelling	Fan	Respect
Compliment	Freedom	Retain
Contemplate	Generate	Review
Context	Grow	Role-model
Cultivate	Guard	Seek
Deepen	Habit	Smart

Delight	Honor	Spark
Demonstrate	Increase	Steps
Detect	Inspire	Strengthen
Develop	Introduce	Stretch
Diligence	Invest	Surprise
Discover	Keep alive	Sustain
Effort	Make time for	Thrill
Empower	Marvel	Thrive

[4]

Thoughts from Dr. Kathy and Tina Hollenbeck

Dr. Kathy   Tina Hollenbeck   Brad Sargent

Tina Hollenbeck has contributed to the Celebrate Kids email newsletter with a column in every issue for many years. She and Kathy wrote a series of columns about the genius qualities in 2013, and the response was so positive that we decided to compile those into this booklet with the added information, written by Brad Sargent, to further help you. (Brad Sargent has worked with Kathy on numerous writing and thinking projects since the mid-1990s.)

We'll share Dr. Armstrong's definitions and discuss each quality in turn and hope to inspire you to make room for them all within yourself and in the lives of the children and teens you influence. We're very excited about the impact this understanding can have! Just as we know far too many folks who've bought the lie that they're not "smart," so, too, we see almost every day how we deny or minimize the genius qualities in ourselves and in our kids. That's a tragic moral crime, in our opinion.

She's Brighter Than She Thinks – Dr. Kathy

At a meeting last week, one particular woman consistently made relevant and insightful comments. Yet, when two or three of us affirmed her and actually called her wise and smart, she became embarrassed and tried hard to dismiss our beliefs.

Because of how this woman shared her ideas, we were easily attentive. Yet, she didn't believe she was wise.

She could convince a fly that I wouldn't be dangerous with a fly swatter in my hands. That's how persuasive she can be. But, she was never manipulative. She's smarter than she thinks.

Sometimes I would catch this woman listening to someone else and she looked like she was about to burst. Sometimes it was because she had something to contribute. Sometimes her face just lit up. Yet, she didn't think she's wise.

I grieve how limited the words "smart" and "wise" have been defined by too many people. Sometimes people like this woman stop trying to contribute. They stop showing up for life. They stop believing. That sure is true of children.

This woman not only demonstrated multiple different smarts while at the meeting, she demonstrated great use of several genius qualities. But, I have a feeling if she didn't believe she was smart or wise, she sure couldn't be convinced she's a genius. I think I'll try sometime, though. We need to call out of people their best.

The Possibilities are Endless – Tina

If you've heard Dr. Kathy speak or have read her **8 Great Smarts** book, you know that every human being is smart in at least eight different ways. You know that a few of the eight smarts stand out as your top strengths and that the same is true of every other person, with the combination of "top smarts" varying from individual to individual. You know each smart can be awakened …or paralyzed. You remember that you – or your child ¬– can, when necessary, learn to pull up and utilize a smart that isn't a top strength. And you understand that we must each be smart with our smarts.

But did you know that many of those same truths apply to the 12 Genius Qualities? Yes, each and every person possesses some measure of each genius trait. As adults, we probably each favor just a few in our daily lives, perhaps because some of the others have been squelched in some way. But it's possible to increase the expression of all 12 of these traits in our lives – and in the lives of our children – and to use them for good purposes each and every day.

So if I can do anything in my writings to help you identify the traits within yourself and in your kids and to encourage you to stop shutting them down and start growing them, I will have been richly rewarded. Please don't doubt your God-given genius or whether your kids have it; give us some time to make our case.

And in the meantime, remember Thomas Edison, who was basically expelled from elementary school when the teacher told his mother he was "retarded" and unteachable. I don't know what happened in that school, but we all know Thomas was obviously a bona fide genius. So, obviously, his parents did something to awaken and inspire his genius qualities. And if that was possible for Thomas – someone who'd nearly had his genius snuffed out – it's possible for you and your kids, too.

With these 12 qualities in action, the possibilities truly are endless. We're so glad you're on this journey with us, and hope you'll find something even today to awaken any of your genius qualities that are dormant, and develop those that have been activated!

[5]

#1 Curiosity

"To ask questions that others judge as irrelevant." [1]

Disobedience or Discovery? – Dr. Kathy

Are your children **curious**? If they are, they have a genius quality. Great! Dr. Armstrong defines curiosity as "asking questions that others judge as irrelevant." Of course, we want children to ask any type of question. That's better than not asking. But, in the context of geniuses, curiosity shows up in questions that others wouldn't bother asking.

In addition to asking questions to satisfy their curiosity, which Tina writes about next, look for other ways your children's curiosity shows up.

- Do they dig in the dirt just to see what's there?
- Do they touch things you ask them not to?
- Do they take things apart because they want to know how they work?
- Do they try using new words, partly to see how you'll react?

Have they tried painting with Kool-Aid because they like the colors and want to see if it works? Several of these examples appear to be rooted in disobedience, don't they?

What if I suggested they're rooted in the genius quality of curiosity instead? Think about this as you read about each of these 12 qualities: We can quickly shut down children's genius qualities if we are very negative every time they experiment.

We need to teach obedience, expect obedience, and react to disobedience without paralyzing children's curiosity. It's a genius quality they're displaying and developing!

Questions, Questions – Tina

Why are crab apples called that?
When were glasses first invented?
If you could be any color of the rainbow, what would you want to be and why?
If you had two extra ears, where would you put them?
Do caterpillars ever trip when they're walking?
If God is big enough to know and see everything, how can He be small enough to fit in our hearts?

As a parent or teacher, you surely hear questions like this every day – many times a day. In fact, as one friend recently remarked, "[Kids] ask so much all the time!" And the breadth and depth of their questions is simply amazing.

Of course, we're busy and we're human, so we can easily tire of children's questions. In fact, when my girls are in a particularly chatty mood, I sometimes long for bedtime just so my ears can get a bit of a rest.

And it's okay to set some boundaries – to ask for silence at particular times or to request that they sometimes write down their questions or research the answers on their own instead of verbalizing queries moment by moment. But we need to guard against being so critical of the questions that we paralyze kids' curiosity.

After all, curiosity – the ability to ponder and wonder – is one of the 12 Genius Qualities. And allowing children to express their curiosity by asking questions is a key means by which we encourage that quality within them.

My 12-year old daughter and I have a nightly "check-in" routine in which I lay down with her for a few minutes shortly after she turns out the lights for the evening. What started as a way to ease her anxiety about insomnia she's since overcome has morphed into an opportunity for mother-daughter bonding. And as part of the routine, she asks four questions about anything on her mind at the time. Sometimes she wants to know about my childhood. Other times she asks about little things like caterpillar legs, and occasionally she ponders deep philosophical questions. I always share my perspective, but sometimes we come to the conclusion that we don't know the answers – so we might need to research them the next day or acknowledge that a few questions are rather unanswerable.

But the point is not the answers. Rather, it's the asking – the chance for her to stretch her "curiosity muscles" – that matters. Of course, there are times when I'd prefer to give my ears a rest sooner each evening – and sometimes I'm so tired I ask her to narrow it down to one or two questions. But giving her at least one guaranteed opportunity each day to ask questions has been one of the best tools upon which I've stumbled for growing her God-given curiosity.

"Staying curious keeps the world from shrinking."

Cameron Crabtree

[6]

#2 Playfulness

"An
Attitude
toward
life." [2]

Excellent Experimentation to Temporarily Reinvent Reality – Dr. Kathy

In our last chapter, curiosity was the genius quality we highlighted. Did knowing that geniuses are curious cause you to respond to your children differently when noticing their curiosity? Did you notice it more often and celebrate it? We hope so.

Playfulness is another quality Dr. Armstrong noticed geniuses have in common. It's an attitude toward life. Nothing is ever too serious. They play well.

Even in the middle of work, the mind of the genius will play, experiment, wonder, ponder, and discover. They may appear to not focus because of these qualities.

Play comes easily and is a natural part of their day. With others, there's an easy give-and-take. It's one fun way we translate our curious questions into experiments with possible answers. It's how much of the world around us and in us can be discovered and understood.

As playful geniuses walk through life, these words might describe them: frisky, whimsical, comical, spirited, fond of fun, lighthearted, merry, perky, gentle. Do these words describe any children or teens you know – or adults, too, for that matter? Do they describe you? It's never too late to develop a latent sense of fun in ourselves, and never too early to fan that spark in others.

Watch this week to see if your kids get into trouble because they're playful. Do they play with their food? Not stay serious as long as you'd like when having a discussion? Imagine, create, and discover what you'd like them to just leave alone?

What are some positive ways to respond to playful geniuses?

Let Them Play – Tina

My daughters and I recently spent the afternoon with good friends. While the other mom and I enjoyed catching up with the happenings in each other's lives, the kids played, alternating between the yard and the basement. They started out with a variety of improvised Barbie games. The three girls included the lone boy by giving him the vintage GI Joe my girls had toted with them. Then they played a round of soccer before heading to the basement.

When I came to tell them it was nearly time to go, I found the entire room in disarray and each child decked out from head to toe. Later, my daughters explained that they'd all donned dress-up clothes and spent their time making up random games in which each played various parts, focusing on storylines set in the medieval era. And it was clear when I came down that all four could have continued on, unabated, for another couple of hours if we'd let them.

The kids are 10½, 11, 12, and almost 13. They never complained of boredom or asked to plunk down in front of a movie or video game. And, though my friend and I would be the first to admit that we've made plenty of parenting mistakes, engaging in imaginative play has always been the case for our kids. They've always enjoyed it, and still do despite how rapidly each is careening toward adolescence.

This wasn't something my friend and I necessarily planned. But in hindsight we can see that − by providing a variety of simple, non-electronic toys, by carving out daily time for play, and by limiting our kids' media consumption − we each ended up creating an environment that has fostered a love of creative, productive play in them even now.

It's not that we're discouraging them from "growing up." In fact, my friend and I are both working diligently to help our kids mature toward a healthy, responsible adulthood. But we've always provided time, space, and opportunity for playfulness. Because of that, we see them retaining childlike wonder, joy, and creativity even as they grow out of childish behavior.

I grieve when I see primary-aged children and even preschoolers glued to iPads and Kindles, which numb them from discovering their own innate creativity. I lament the overscheduled lives some families lead – in which the children are shuttled from one organized activity to another. Such busyness eliminates the possibility of kids having daily unstructured time in which to play as their imaginations dictate. There is a time and place for activities and technology. But if we want our kids to develop the genius quality of playfulness, we must let them play – really play – instead of us, schedules, or gadgets merely entertaining and occupying them.

"The reluctance to put away childish things may be a requirement of genius."

Rebecca Pepper Sinkler

[7]

#3 Imagination

"To close their eyes and 'see' ..."[3]

A Jurassic Spark – Dr. Kathy

Imagination is another genius quality. It's more present in children than adults because, as Dr. Armstrong points out, children are more apt to close their eyes and see all sorts of images. Although adults can still imagine, we're more apt to close our eyes and see reality.

What may be my all-time favorite evidence that young children are imaginative came from a young boy that I'll call Brent. At the end of a recent day, Brent's parents asked him, "What was your favorite thing we did today?"

Without skipping a beat and as confident as can be, he declared, "We built toy dinosaurs!"

But actually, they didn't. And Brent's parents told me he usually answers this question with something they ***didn't*** do. It's not that Brent doesn't like anything he actually does. His imagination is sometimes just better.

We can give kids time to imagine. We can ask them what they see in their mind's eye. We can listen to their made-up stories. We can encourage imaginative play. We can join them to keep ***our*** imagination alive, too – imagine that!

Time and Opportunity – Tina

Have you ever watched or listened to your children play and wished you could see the inner workings of their brains? I feel that way often about my daughters, but recently I was even more curious than usual.

My 11-year old took quite a bit of time one day to carefully arrange many of her paper dolls on the kitchen table. Once they were set, I expected her to invite her sister to play with her or to begin acting out scenes on her own. But to my surprise she didn't do either. Instead, she appeared merely to stare at the dolls, occasionally picking up one or another and moving it to a different location on the table.

I continued with my work around the house, but after more than an hour of this, I couldn't contain my curiosity any longer and finally asked, "Are you going to play, Abigail, or are you just looking at them today?"

With a demure but confident smile, she answered, "I am playing. I'm imagining each doll's dialogue in my head as they interact with each other. It's really fun."

On the one hand, that didn't surprise me one bit; Abigail has always had a very active imagination. But on the other hand, it floored me to know she was creating complex scenarios all *in her head*.

And she's not the only one who does it. In fact, I would daresay that *most* children can and do engage their imaginations – and the picture-smart part of their brain – in similar ways if given the time and opportunity.

But do we really provide either? Do we allow children to "make their own fun" with simple toys and supplies that stretch their imaginations? Do we grant them unstructured time that they must discover how to fill productively? Or do we, instead, program and plan their every waking minute and fill their rooms with toys that beep and buzz and talk at them, telling them what to think and feel?

There's a place in each child's life for organized activity. And it's okay for kids to occasionally "be entertained" – via apps or websites or TV. But we make a serious mistake if we think that days overflowing with technology and scheduled "enrichment" will give our kids a leg-up in life. Children need to develop their imaginations and the other genius qualities in order to ultimately lead productive, fulfilled lives. So we need to do what it takes to build that into them from an early age. We need to give them the time and opportunity to create within their own heads.

"Perhaps imagination is only intelligence having fun."

George Scialabba

[8]

#4 Creativity

"To give birth to new ways of looking at things."[4]

Novel Approaches to Any Old Problem –
Dr. Kathy

One of the most important things we must understand about creativity is that it's more – much more – than only an ability that shows up in art class. That's how we defined it in the old days. We must free creativity from only the realm of art and put it everywhere. Kids have an openness to see things adults often can't see, or can't see in the same way. That's creativity – looking at things in new ways. This gift shows up as all kinds of inventiveness.

Are your kids creative with systems? Have they watched you do something and then made suggestions to increase efficiency?

Are your kids creative with questions? Have they asked about things you've never thought to ask about? A child looked at me once, and asked, "Since cows eat green grass, how come milk is white?"

Maybe you have a son creative with space. Does he put things in places that are perfect, but you never thought of? Does he design places that are ideal and comfortable for his younger sisters?

Some kids are creative with colors and enjoy showing you the purple cat they drew or the blue apple they painted. Then, they work to convince you blue apples would taste better than red or yellow ones do.

Watch for creativity. Enjoy what new-to-you things you see and enter into conversations to keep creativity alive. Kids are born with this ability. If we're not careful, we can quickly shut it down. Can you predict how? Watch and listen and see what you notice. Then see what ... creative ... new ways of promoting creativity you can start to see in yourself and others, and use!

A Launchpad to Creativity -Tina

Many years ago, I read an article that recommended reading aloud to children every day of their lives – from the very beginning (maybe even in utero) until the day they leave for college or their own apartments.

Sadly, I don't think enough parents read aloud to even their young children these days, let alone to kids who've learned to read on their own. In fact, I've even heard occasional comments from parents thrilled that their children have learned to read – no matter how cursorily – because it means they'll "finally" get back all the time they'd been "losing" each day reading to them.

After seeing that article, though, I started reading aloud at least a few days a week to my middle-school students. And when I transferred to teaching high school, I continued the read-aloud practice with my students there. I wondered if they'd feel I was treating them like "babies" – I had mixed-grade classes, including plenty of 18-year old seniors. But, they enjoyed it, often asking me to read more than one chapter a day. And it wasn't because it got them out of work. Despite our 10- to 15-minutes of read-aloud time a few days a week, I didn't decrease my classroom expectations at all.

When I left classroom teaching to stay home with my newborn daughter, I determined that daily read-alouds would be a priority throughout my children's lives. And, with the help of my book-loving husband, I've maintained the practice even as my girls approach adolescence.

In fact, it's been through seeing my kids' development in ways not possible with my students that I've grasped the importance of the habit. You see, as much as we've attempted to develop a rich learning environment for our children – they took their first plane ride when they were mere toddlers – we're not able to physically visit every country of the world. Not even close. And, of course, we couldn't time-travel even if we were independently wealthy. But books truly do open up the world – across space and time.

I've seen time and again how my children have latched onto aspects of various books we've read and have then synthesized those ideas into something new during a doll or play-acting game of their own creation. Just the other day, they created a storyline with their Barbies that would "solve racism." Inevitably, the seeds of their ideas have come from books – those they read on their own but also plenty we've read to them.

If you've not been in the habit of reading to your older children or students, introducing the practice will necessitate some scheduling adjustments. But, of course, anything worth doing requires effort. In terms of where to start, just choose something a little above your children's independent reading level and begin. There are great book resource lists by Jim Trelease in **The Read-Aloud Handbook** and by Gladys Hunt and Barbara Hampton in **Read for Your Life: Turning Teens**

into Readers. If you want to build the genius quality of creativity into your kids, reading aloud to them is a perfect launching pad. (And even some graphic novels based on classic tales can introduce them to great themes from world literature!)

"I saw the angel in the marble and carved until I set him free."

Michelangelo

[9]

#5 Wonder

"Natural astonishment about
the world"[5]

Finding What's Underneath and Beyond the Ordinary – Dr. Kathy

Vacationing with my parents, brother, and extended family at Fish Lake near Wautoma, Wisconsin, was an annual tradition. I smile just thinking about it.

Swimming was a big part of our joy. We wondered how far we could swim without stopping to rest and then we'd swim to find out. We wondered how long we could float, who could float the longest, and then we did it to find out.

We had many fishing contests. Would my brother, dad, and I catch more fish from our boat and our special spot than my uncle and cousins would catch from theirs? We wondered, we went fishing, then we found out.

My mom and my aunt always walked us to an old cemetery on a cloudy day. We examined tombstones and wondered about the people buried there. We made up stories and wondered if we were right.

We had time to wonder. We had people to wonder with. We explored. We tried things. We responded with wonder.

It's a verb … "I wonder how deep the sand goes." And, an emotional response … "Wow! It goes and goes forever!"

We don't have to be out-of-doors to express wonder about the world. We can engage it anywhere. Even at home, we can wonder and we can help our kids wonder. We can be surprised; not take everything for granted; and make time to question, sit, and observe. We can *not* quickly answer kids' questions if it would be better for them to explore and figure some things out on their own.

Today, go on a vacation or staycation from your busy, typical, grade-book existence and wonder.

Like a Baby – Tina

I regularly babysit a two-year old girl. And I spent the last couple weeks of August caring for her almost-seven-year-old sister, as well as another friend's one-year-old daughter. Adding in my own two girls, we had a house overflowing with estrogen!

But the place was also bursting with wonder. It was constantly obvious in the baby, whose eyes grew wide with interest every time she picked up a new toy. Whether noting what happened when she banged two sorting cups together, "talking" to a Little People figurine she turned over and over in her hands, or discovering the knobs and buttons on a toy barn, her wonder about everything was clear.

Likewise with the two-year old, who revels in paging carefully through picture books and making long lines of toy dishes, blocks, and Mr. Potato Head parts. It's clear that she's regularly fascinated by the world around her, too.

With older kids and adults, though, wonder is often more difficult to elicit and detect. Either we're preoccupied with necessary daily tasks – from schoolwork to laundry to keeping up with emails – or we become discouraged and skeptical because of the all-too-ugly life realities that go unnoticed by young children.

But watching the baby and toddler in my care, I was reminded of wonder and felt challenged to purposefully direct myself and the older children toward it. So I asked each of the older girls to tell me about one thing that makes her think, "Wow!"

Young Anna, who will turn seven in a month, smiled and promptly said, "Airplanes. I saw one right up close once, and I saw another one landing. It was really close to the ground and it was really big."

Eleven-year old Abigail replied, "The amazing animals God made. Like the duck-billed platypus. That's a sign of God's sense of humor!"

Twelve-year old Rachel, herself an artist, had to think for a few moments, but she finally said, "Art. Michelangelo."

And what amazes me is noticing at random moments the unique wiring of each child's mind and heart as they all grow and develop into who God means for each to be. I really do regularly marvel at their creativity that's innate, the notions they contemplate, and the skills they demonstrate. On a more grown-up level, it's all an extension of the baby studying the details of her own moving fingers.

Having wonder – a natural astonishment about the world – is an inherent human genius quality. Anyone who's observed babies and toddlers must acknowledge that. Thus, we don't really need to find ways to develop it. Rather, what older kids

– and adults – need in this case is a commitment to keeping our inborn wonder alive and active.

So what can you do today to awaken wonder in yourself and the kids in your care?

"We are perishing for want of wonder, not for want of wonders."

G.K. Chesterton

[10]

#6 Wisdom

"[T]o experience the wonder the world directly, without the blinders of preconceptions and clichés."[6]

of

Solution- Oriented Analysis and Synthesis about a Situation – Dr. Kathy

So far, we've looked at the genius qualities of curiosity, playfulness, imagination, creativity, and wonder.

How do these qualities connect with and reinforce each other?

Which one(s) have you most liked, or most worked on developing further since reading this booklet?

Which one(s) do you most see being nourished and flourishing in your children or teens? Why do you think that is?

The sixth quality identified by Dr. Armstrong is wisdom. Wisdom isn't intelligence and it's not the accumulation of knowledge. What is it? Read what Tina says about "Wisdom Words." I'll be shocked if you don't want your children and students to have this quality.

If you've reflected on which of these qualities are strengths for your children, it's possible you've noticed they've declined through the years. Are they less creative than they used to be? Do they not imagine as much as they used to? Have you wondered what's happened?

There are many ways that genius qualities get shut down. But be encouraged. The way we live our lives and the decisions we make help our children develop these important qualities. And, later in this series, I'll share how the attributes can be reawakened if they've been stifled.

You may not exactly have realized it while you were reading the above, but I did a *review* of previous information and knowledge, in part by using questions, plus a *preview* of what's to come. Reviews, questions, and previews are positive ways to spark analysis and synthesis of details that we've learned already and to get us ready to learn more that we can process and apply later. So, actually, these are parts in wisdom-making and application-building processes! What other ideas can you generate with your kids about working toward wisdom?

Wisdom Words – Tina

No doubt about it, we live in a knowledge-saturated culture. We can easily access information about any conceivable topic

24/7/365, usually with only one or two clicks of a mouse or thumb. And as a result, we tend to believe we are a wise people. After all, if wisdom and knowledge are synonymous, our society is replete with it.

The problem is that wisdom and knowledge are not synonyms. Knowledge is information – facts and opinions we've already learned or can discover about a topic. As a culture, we're overwhelmed with an ability to gain knowledge. But knowledge is only one part of wisdom.

From the beginning of time and across cultures, wisdom has actually been defined as "*applied* knowledge." Thus, wisdom entails much more than simple acquisition of information. In fact, in order to be wise, a person must take two crucial steps beyond gaining knowledge:
1. *Parse* through all the information to discover the nuggets of *truth* therein, discarding the rest;
2. *Choose* to *apply* that truth to one's life in order to achieve a specific goal or purpose.

When we look at it that way, it's fair to say that our culture – and many of us individually – are actually foolish most of the time. For one thing, we don't relish taking the time to weed through information. We also live in a time when we've been (incorrectly) led to believe that truth is relative, not absolute; thus, we struggle to find truth even when we seek it. And, finally, we have a hard time wanting to diligently work toward the changes that application of truth would necessitate, often preferring the path of least resistance instead.

But if we don't apply the truths found within the knowledge at our fingertips, we cannot gain wisdom. If we choose to discount wisdom in our own lives, we cannot adequately facilitate its acquisition in our children. And, chillingly, the prophet Hosea told us the end result of that decision when he warned that, "[the] people perish from a lack of wisdom."

Obviously, that concept warrants serious consideration in our own lives as adults. And we can't legitimately expect our children to be wise if we're unwilling to engage in the process ourselves. "Do as I say, not as I do" falls flat every time. But it's crucial for our kids and for our culture that we help children grow toward wisdom with us; we can't wait until we "have it all together" before we begin to address it with our children.

One simple technique we can use in many situations with our kids is to actively walk them through wisdom-growing questions:

1. What do you **know** about this situation?
2. Of everything you know, what one or two **truths** can you pull out?
3. How can you put that truth **into practice** right now?
4. What can I do to help?

Working through this process will cause kids to pause and think, plus role model that they don't always have to seek wisdom alone. Doing it on a regular basis will develop in them a habit of mind that enables them to begin asking themselves these questions automatically, and that will grow them toward wisdom over time. Given Hosea's words as well as the truth that wisdom is a genius quality, isn't that something we'd want to do?

"Knowledge comes, but wisdom lingers."

Alfred Lord Tennyson

[11]

#7 Inventiveness

"A 'hands-on' creativity; creating new things from known things."[7]

Concrete Solutions to Pressing Problems –
Dr. Kathy

If you had predicted what was on this genius list after only reading the title, I bet you might have included "inventiveness." When thinking about geniuses, we often think of those who invented many things or important things we can't imagine living without.

Ben Franklin comes to mind. In addition to drafting the Declaration of Independence and publishing newspapers, he invented the Franklin stove, bifocals, and the lightning rod. He established or greatly improved libraries, public hospitals, mutual insurance companies, and volunteer fire departments. He founded the post office. You and your children could each choose which invention of his is the most important and try to convince the others you're right.

What if you went through your kitchen listing all the things you see that were invented? Choose which one you think is the most important – or most unusual – and list reasons. You could choose an invention from years ago and one that's more current. For instance, the United Kingdom's National Academy of Science named the refrigerator, pasteurized milk, and the tin can in the top 20 food/kitchen inventions of all time.

George Washington Carver was an agricultural chemist who invented 300 uses for peanuts. Enjoy some peanuts with your children and name what inventions of his you can. Then use research tools to discover others. It's an amazing list!

Henry Ford invented the assembly line for automobile manufacturing. Use an assembly line with your children to make something. (Perhaps peanut butter and jelly sandwiches.) You could discuss all the advantages of making things this way. Maybe there's a manufacturing plant in your area you could tour so your children could see an assembly line in action.

Here's another discussion to have: What do you wish someone would invent? What problem would it lessen or solve? What do your children wish could be invented? Why not them?

Parenting Toward Inventiveness – Tina

I enjoy being organized. I gravitate toward ordering my world, naturally creating places for everything and keeping it all there.

I'm grateful, though, that mentors in my early years as a mom convinced me that keeping strict order and maximizing a child's potential don't necessarily mix. If I hadn't accepted that truth, I'm sure I'd have been the mom following her kids around, picking up each toy the minute one of them appeared to be done with it.

I didn't abandon organization. But I put it in its proper place, allowing my kids to freely play all throughout the day – which is, of course, how young children learn – and typically picking up just once each evening. I sometimes felt overwhelmed by the apparent "clutter." But that arrangement allowed my kids to be creative and inventive, using each toy in several different ways each day as they encountered it at different times.

As they got older, both girls showed a penchant for crafting and building. And it wasn't long before they realized they could turn cardboard boxes into works of art and architecture. Of course, one girl's craft spawned an idea in her sister, such that it sometimes seemed they were asking for multiple boxes every day.

I had the boxes; as an organizer, I had a designated "box nook" in my basement under the laundry table. (Even we organizers can get inventive to solve our problems!) I saved boxes throughout the year, planning to use them to hold Christmas presents. But I stressed about the continual box requests. For one thing, what would I use at Christmas if the girls used up all my boxes? And, secondly, where would we keep the many, lovely – often quite large – finished projects? They couldn't be stacked in the box nook once they'd been cut up and taped into new configurations. Instead, they were given new homes, spread throughout the entire second level of our house and, often enough, even in our living room so the girls could invent new games with them each day. The designs were very clever, but they messed with my sense of organization.

Thankfully, though, I remembered that houses are meant to be lived in; they are not museums. And if I wanted my kids to become increasingly inventive, I had to provide them with space and materials with which to get their hands busy ... and dirty. We could still make room for organization – the girls and

I worked together to devise a system for "super-cleaning" when necessary – but we determined that enabling and empowering our kids to express their natural desires to make new things was more important than perfect order.

Kids need time and space and "stuff" to invent with. Are you contributing to the process?

"To invent, you need a good imagination and a pile of junk."

Thomas A. Edison

[12]

#8 Vitality

"Being awake
to your senses,
totally and
immediately
responsive
to the
environment,
and actively
engaged in
each and every
moment"[8]

The Spark for the Fire of Genius – Dr. Kathy

Dr. Tom Armstrong, who compiled this list of genius qualities we're sharing, writes that "vitality is the essential spark of genius." Therefore, it's certainly one we'd want to encourage in the children and teens we influence.

As Tina will point out, young children may naturally have this quality. But, it dies. Do we cause it to die? We may. It's not easy for us when our children are actively engaged in each and every moment. Their liveliness, intensity, and fervor can exhaust us. Their constant comments or questions about what they observe may frustrate us.

But, that's what makes it a genius quality. Their mental energy keeps them thinking. They see what others haven't noticed. They hear things with fresh ears. It's what allows them to discover what could be improved or invented from scratch.

So, let's choose to not squelch their enthusiasm – even if we have to redirect it sometimes.

Meanwhile, what about you? Have you realized, like me, that you're not awake to everything around you? Join me in committing to reawakening this quality in yourself. I'm going to slow down a bit and notice more. Vitality is what will lead to wonder. I'm going to choose to experience more of life with all five senses. I want to assume less and be open to new insights more.

Not only will vitality add to our thinking power. Choosing to process life with it will help us better understand children who naturally have this quality and may get into trouble as a result.

Time for Vitality – Tina

We spend a great deal of time and energy helping our children grow beyond childish behavior and ideas. And rightfully so. After all, we want them to mature emotionally and relationally as they approach adulthood. But is there any way in which we should encourage them to remain like little children – and even strive for that ourselves?

In matters of faith, of course, Jesus reminds us in each of the Gospels (i.e., Matthew 18.3) to trust Him as little children. And another way in which we should be child-like (not childish) is in terms of the genius quality of vitality.

"Vitality" in this context means, "being awake to one's senses and totally and immediately responsive." And little children – babies, toddlers, and preschoolers – are truly the ideal models of this trait. They immediately and quite naturally respond to what impacts their senses, and they demonstrate an innate desire to explore what they see, hear, smell, touch, and taste.

The precious two-year old I babysit personifies this. She's on the go from the moment she walks into my house each morning until her mom picks her up before lunch. First, she hurries to find my cats so she can pet them, and then she's off to our playroom to see what new toys I've set out for the day. From there, she chooses one thing or another throughout the morning – sometimes the toy food and dishes, other times the puzzles or Little People, and always the books – rotating among them as her interests lead. When we go outside, she alternately revels in the wind on her face as we push her on a swing, gets engrossed in sandbox digging, or embarks on a mission to collect leaves and sticks. We don't need to instruct her to be interested in everything around her; she just is.

Sadly, too many children lose such vitality as they get older, and it's exceedingly rare to find it in adults. Instead, we become so consumed with busy schedules and completing "important" tasks that we dismiss many natural opportunities to discover and learn. We allow ourselves to become "human doings" instead of deepen ourselves as "human beings."

And that's really a terrible infection. Of course, working productively is important. But if we – or our children – live on a treadmill of busyness, we hurry through each day without enjoying anything. We become overtired and overwrought. We lose our ability to think creatively and to treasure simple pleasures.

The antidote is time. We need to choose to make time in our lives – and in the lives of our children – to be like toddlers. Time to set aside the to-do list. Time, in fact, when we needn't "do" anything in particular. Time to watch, think, and feel.

We don't dismiss our need to accomplish our work – whatever it is. We simply acknowledge that, in order to be vital human beings, we also need time to just "be." Striking the balance can be tricky. But it's necessary for our well-being and for that of the kids in our care.

"Vitality shows in not only the ability to persist but the ability to start over."

F. Scott Fitzgerald

[13]

#9 Sensitivity

"The incredible openness
that children have
to the world"[9]

It's Impressive to Stay Impressionable – Dr. Kathy

I agree with Dr. Armstrong's definition. Children tend to be more open than adults in both mind and heart, and in their five senses. They don't have as many preconceived notions of how things are supposed to be or work. Children don't have to get out of a box because they're not in one to begin with. Some adults not only live in a box; they have the lid shut.

I definitely lived that way for a long time. I liked knowing what I knew and I didn't mind not knowing what I didn't know. I thought about what I wanted to and left the rest alone. I didn't naturally engage my heart when thinking.

What happened to change me? I began associating with open, sensitive people. I saw and liked their freedom, joy, and sensitivity to other people's ideas and feelings. They felt other people's feelings and also reacted to ideas with their own feelings. I learned engaging the heart was a good thing that didn't have to interfere with my thoughts. (Yes, I used to think it would.) I learned I could trust these friends with my observations and feelings. I, therefore, gained experience and confidence.

I'm grateful because I've become a better person from this. And I find other genius qualities are easier to use when I'm sensitive to what's going on around me, impressionable to people, places, and experiences. I agree with Dr. Armstrong: Sensitivity makes life more vivid. Get out of your box or help someone else move beyond their self-imposed boundaries or those forced upon them by others. Lift the lid. Try it. Tina and I can't be the only two who have needed to make changes.

Sensitivity – Don't Steal or Kill the Gift – Tina

"You are such a baby!"

"Just get over it."

"Stop being so sensitive!"

I heard those kinds of admonitions from every adult in my life and many peers as well. And, sadly, though I faced multiple situations that would legitimately strike fear and even terror into the heart of any child, I listened all too well. By the time I was in high school, I'd become so adept at stifling any "negative" feelings that others considered me stoic, tough, and unapproachable. In fact, a friend I met as a college freshman later told me that he could practically see the thick, looming, self-protective wall I'd built around myself.

I had no intentions of tearing down that wall. I wasn't happy, of course. But since I'd learned that expressing my feelings garnered ridicule and verbal assault, burying – and, I'd hoped, killing – my sensitivity would at least keep me "safe."

Thankfully, the Lord had other ideas, and He worked through a number of people to redeem me from that bondage. But it was a terrifying process because the first feeling I recovered was anger – in fact, a rage so overwhelming at times I felt sure it would consume me. Then I regained sadness, but it came in the form of chronic, debilitating despair that I feared would swallow me up. I desperately wanted to stop and latch onto the safe numbness I'd cultivated as a youth, but God wouldn't let me turn back. And finally – blessedly – the scary feelings leveled off and I recovered joy as well. But it took a long time.

I now understand that sensitivity is an ability to feel deeply from along the whole spectrum of emotions, not the negative quality our culture so often portrays it to be. It is a gift and a genius quality. And I've determined to cultivate it in my daughters. So when we laugh, we give it everything we've got. When they're angry, I don't tell them to get over it; instead, I help them learn to express it appropriately and walk all the way through it to the other side. And when they're sad, I don't shush them. Instead, I hold them tightly and let them cry it out, sobbing for as long as it takes to feel the release I know will always eventually come.

Plus, contrary to popular opinion, accepting and encouraging their sensitivity hasn't turned them into selfish narcissists. Actually, by allowing them to experience and work through – not deny – their own feelings, my kids have been able to develop a security that allows them to take their eyes off of themselves. And, because they haven't had to build up a wall of self-protection, they're able to see and reach out to others in the spirit of true, authentic relationship.

I now cry – in happy and sad situations – at the drop of a hat. But I had to rediscover the sensitivity that was stolen from me and blocked by me. How much better for our kids if they never lose it in the first place?

**"The most important innovators often don't need any technologies –
just imagination and acute sensitivity to people's needs."**

Geoff Mulgan

[14]

#10 Flexibility

"The ability of children to make fluid associations."[10]

No Barriers to the Fluid Mind – Dr. Kathy

As with the other nine genius qualities we've written about, we don't want to squelch children's flexible thinking. Rather, we need to do what we can to awaken and strengthen it. Of course, our kids need to exercise self-control and obedience so they don't get into trouble with their flexibility, curiosity, or inventiveness.

There are times when our children or students must stay focused and concentrate on one thing at a time. But, when moving between topics and ideas won't interfere with what needs to be accomplished, we should encourage that in them. Flexibility is like a flash-flood of water: inevitably it finds its way in, around, or through all kinds of seeming barriers. Similarly, when people apply fluidity and flexibility, they experiment with, explore, and eventually see through to new ways of thinking and doing. Thus, exercising flexible thinking can contribute to children's successful accomplishments and maybe even increase their efficiency.

Using a theme approach is one way to increase flexible thinking as we and our children engage with content that's related even if it cuts across different academic areas. This approach can also keep things more interesting. For instance, have you ever had the great pleasure of reading *Charlotte's Web* to children? It could spawn all kinds of units of study:

- English: The "ch" sound like in "Charlotte" versus as in "change," and vocabulary development such as asking what a spider web and the world wide web have in common – why is "web" used for both – and how is a cobweb different from a spider web?
- Science/Nutrition: How are pigs cared for on family farms and by big companies? What are all the food products we enjoy from them? How are spiders help-ful?
- Social studies: Compare and contrast farm life versus city life.
- Math: Compare weights of different animals, or the sizes of different farms.

A second way to increase flexible thinking is to listen more carefully to children's questions that initially appear to be ir-relevant. Perhaps they're actually connecting content in unu-sual ways you wouldn't have thought of. Honoring their questions is a great way to support their flexible thinking. Ask what made them think of the question. Affirm them. Then work with them to find answers.

Whatever it Takes – Tina

One of the blessings of homeschooling is its rather natural predisposition toward helping kids develop the genius quality of flexibility. For example, non-traditional homeschooling methodologies encourage and allow children to read about and study topics of personal interest well beyond the few paragraphs found in a textbook. Additionally, a homeschooling family has more freedom to go off on "rabbit trails" of interest that may come to light while reading textbooks. And, because the one-on-one tutoring inherent in homeschooling allows kids to complete standard academic studies in much less time each day, they have more free time for exploring personal interests and passions. This enables their developing myriad "fluid associations" as they explore particular topics on their own.

Before my kids were born, I spent nine years as a classroom teacher, and I remember the pace and the pressure and the dry, uninspiring nature of most mainstream textbooks. Though unusual even then, I was given the freedom to develop and use a very successful readers/writers workshop format that encouraged flexibility in my students' thinking and studying. However, I realize things are much tougher now because of questionable standardization efforts like the common core and undue emphasis on high-stakes testing. None of that leaves room for flexibility. I know the current situation grieves the hearts of caring teachers who want to meet kids' real needs.

So does such a reality mean kids attending traditional school can't develop the important genius quality of flexibility? Of course not. But because it's not built into the system, teachers and parents of kids in the schools must make concerted, conscious efforts toward that end. But how?

Teachers, even if you must require your students to read the textbooks, can you find ways to incorporate more projects in lieu of some quizzes and exams? The text can provide a basic overview of information for all. But then each student can also have the freedom to choose from a wide variety of engaging, "living" books for deeper research in order to create interesting, useful projects. In so doing, each student will more easily remember the basic information while also developing those fluid associations through his or her personal study.

Parents, can you guard your children's time? So often we feel we must fill a child's every waking minute with structured activity, and we believe that more and more "enrichment" will help in the future. While that's true to an extent, children really do need unstructured time in order to develop personal interests and to take on individualized learning endeavors for making fluid associations.

Of course, those are just two examples. We as adults who have kids' best interests in mind can brainstorm many more possibilities over time. What's important is to realize kids need to develop this trait of intellectual flexibility and that we need to do whatever it takes to facilitate the process.

"The boldness of asking deep questions may require unforeseen flexibility if we are to accept the answers."

Brian Greene

[15]

#11 Humor

"Looking at things differently;
a trait that breaks us out of ruts and
routines and causes 'aliveness'
to occur."[11]

The Values of Laughter and a Light Touch Toward Life – Dr. Kathy

As you've been reading about genius qualities identified by Dr. Armstrong, how many qualities up to this point have you thought could get kids into trouble – and which ones?

1. Curiosity
2. Playfulness
3. Imagination
4. Creativity
5. Wonder
6. Wisdom
7. Inventiveness
8. Vitality
9. Sensitivity
10. Flexibility

What about this chapter's quality, humor? Oh, yes! ☺

Based on his study of geniuses, Dr. Armstrong defines humor as "a trait that breaks us out of ruts and routines and causes a cackle of excitement or aliveness to occur." I love the word "aliveness." If more learning situations at home, school, and church were described with this word, much more learning would take place.

Getting out of the rut can free all of us to see things different-ly. I may not be the one with the strong sense of humor to get myself and others out of the rut and routine. But I can choose to go with the person who's leading me out of the rut. That's honoring and trusting. When I do, I might just see something I wouldn't have seen otherwise. This is where inventing may occur. We can explore what we're curious about. This "alive-ness" may just give birth to other genius qualities that other-wise get stifled by learning routines.

But, it's hard because so many adults think children need to be controlled and adults need to be in control at all times. We can allow for humor. We shouldn't assume "if you give kids an inch, they'll take a mile." That's what I'm afraid sometimes happens. We're fearful to do anything that might trigger kids' humor. And if we do and they begin to laugh or express their humor in other ways, we're often very quick to stifle it.

Do children with a good sense of humor need character quali-ties so they use their humor well? Absolutely. This is how they'll know the difference between having fun and making fun of someone. This is how they'll become other-centered and aware of how others react constructively or destructively to their humor, rather than just aware of themselves and the attention they're getting. This is what will prepare them to transition back to serious work after the "aliveness break."

What can you do this week and next, at home and/or school, to allow for and even plan for the humor genius quality to be celebrated? I hope you do something that leads to surprising success!

Humor Me – It's About Relationship – Tina

Some days it's hard to see the humor in anything.

News broadcasts bombard us with stories of tragedy in the Philippines, discord in Washington D.C., and teenagers playing the potentially fatal "knockout game" for fun. A friend's child is severely injured in a motorcycle accident, and we can only stand by helplessly as a chronic illness saps the strength of a dearly loved family member. We wonder how we might afford to replace an 18-year old car when expenses continue to rise and salaries don't. We shudder at the thought of the world our children will inherit.

We obviously can't pretend none of that exists; we need to acknowledge it and walk through each reality, day by day. But we can choose to refuse to let it consume us. And humor is one way to avoid being sucked into the vortex of angst we sometimes feel around and within us.

As I was thinking about humor in my family – and remembering my years as a classroom teacher – I realized anew that it occurs in the context of relationship. Thus, I could attempt to explain multiple situations in which my husband and children and I laughed ourselves silly, or times when my students and I bantered and joked with each other. But the humor in the stories would likely fall flat in the retelling because it occurred as we interacted in situations and relationships specific to us. That's why there is truth to the adage, "You kind of had to be there." Particular circumstances were funny because of our understanding of each other and our shared life experiences.

In fact, if we're really engaged in transparent and honest relationships, humor will naturally flow as we share our lives, foibles and all, with each other. Thus, we needn't strive to purposely increase humor in our lives because, important as it is, it cannot be manufactured. Rather, if we see the value of humor to our emotional and intellectual health, we should aim to build and deepen our human relationships, and then humor will grow on its own.

Conversely, if we notice that our days are humorless – that we regularly shuffle through daily tasks and chores with absolutely no enjoyment, happiness, and wonder – we'd do well to examine the state of our relationships. Are we really relating to our spouses and children, or merely coexisting with them? Are we really engaged with our students, or only working through another set of lesson plans? And if we realize we're in relational ruts, will we take responsibility to pull ourselves out?

Sometimes when I realize my daughters and I have gotten too wrapped up in our daily routine, I shake things up. I surprise them by tickling them out of the blue or initiating a silly game of chase. They're 11 and 12, so we don't do either regularly anymore. But that's part of why it's so effective. And after enjoying some good belly laughs together, we feel closer to each other, heartened, and ready to proceed.

What will work like that for your relationships today?

**"Humor is by far the most significant
activity of the human brain."**

Edward de Bono

[16]

#12 Joy

"Comes from deep inside us when a new connection is made, a new insight obtained, a new feat accomplished, or a skill mastered."[12]

Newness That Delights the Soul – Dr. Kathy

When discussing what you enjoy about parenting and teaching, I wonder if you would include what I would. One thing stands out for me – whether when I was teaching second graders; coaching middle schoolers; being a university professor; or doing what I do now to share with parents, teachers, and students. *I love watching people respond when ideas make sense.* It brings them joy, and makes me joyful!

I always have. Do you? Although I taught second graders a long time ago, I can still remember many names and faces and delightful, energizing times as truth made sense to them. They would smile broadly and sometimes come up to me, show me their work, and proclaim, "I got this one right!" They were joyful.

College students responded well to truth. And, as recently as last week, I watched women in my audience respond with the twelfth genius quality: joy. It rose from deep within them as an insight connected to something in their experience.

According to Dr. Armstrong's research, joy is a genius quality. He found it was a common response when people made new connections among ideas, obtained insights, accomplished new feats, and mastered new skills.

Do you see joy in those you influence? It's powerful and deeply motivating, isn't it? Let's commit to teaching, communicating, and parenting to keep genius qualities alive in others.

Curiosity. Playfulness. Imagination. Creativity . Wonder. Wisdom. Inventiveness. Vitality. Sensitivity. Flexibility. Humor. Joy.

Each can be awakened, acknowledged, and strengthened. It's our privilege to be part of that process!

Choosing Joy – Tina

I lived for a season with depression. So, I understand from the distinct contrast between depths of depression and heights of joy how the latter is a genius quality.

When I came out of the depression, I noticed with surprise that everything appeared markedly more vivid than it had before. Colors shone more brightly – whether the hues of autumn leaves or the glow of neon lights. The sounds of birds and cars and voices resonated more clearly. The tastes of spices and the various scents in my environment stood out. The facial features of friends and loved ones seemed more sharply defined. I became "alive" again to interactions with those around me, more fully engaging in relationship with friends and strangers alike. It was like coming out of a long, dark tunnel and bursting forth into Narnia after Aslan's arrival.

Only in hindsight could I see how dull everything had appeared in my depression and how disengaged I'd been from others and from my own soul. In that state, I'd been in survival mode, struggling just to get through each day. I'd been completely uninterested in and unable to accomplish anything creative or compelling. In other words, my God-given genius – joy and the other qualities with which we're all innately gifted – had been paralyzed, locked in a vice grip of emotional dysfunction. As I thawed out of that stupor, my sensitivity, curiosity, and joy woke anew. But I had to come out of it to get there. Of course, emotional dysfunction is one of several factors that shuts down any person's genius qualities. And because the loss of joy saps energy, humor, playfulness, and the rest, perhaps it is one of the main warning signs that something is wrong within the heart of a child or adult.

So, we want to do what we can to maintain joy. But how is that possible in the midst of personal difficulties and societal strife that surround and threaten to engulf us?

We first need to understand the true definition of joy. It is not "happiness." If it were, the scriptural admonition to "count it all joy" (James 1:2) would be cruel. One cannot be "happy" when a job is lost, a house burns to the ground, or a dear loved one is snatched away from this life, and it would be terrible to suggest such a thing. However, we *can* have "joy" in such circumstances – *if* we understand that joy is not the giddy glee of happiness. Instead, it's actually the presence of a deep, internal conviction that all things will eventually work out for good.

People often believe they've lost their joy; I felt that in my depression. But it's not true. I'd actually just become so overwhelmed by temporary circumstances that the natural joy within me was stifled. That's a common and understandable reaction to stress, but I simply didn't realize that until later. Now, though, I understand the dynamics, and I realize I have a choice in the matter. I'll obviously continue to experience events that bring frustration and sadness, and I will, of course, not always be happy. Yet I can choose to refuse to allow my joy to be suffocated, so that it and my other God-given genius qualities might remain viable. In the midst of hurt and tragedy, that takes work. But it's possible and it's worth it.

Do you agree?

"The noblest pleasure is the joy of understanding."

Leonardo da Vinci

[17]

How Genius Qualities Get Shut Down

It's intriguing that Dr. Armstrong devotes as much space in his book to how these 12 Genius Qualities get shut down as to how they get awakened and grow. Clearly, this is important to him. It's not enough to promote what's positive; we need to prevent what's destructive.

There is a ***natural*** neural decrease that starts around age 2 and continues, a sort of "pruning," and then becomes less for adults. That makes the formative years of children and teens crucial for developing the characteristics. But Dr. Armstrong also sees ***unnecessary*** decreases in and depression of these qualities from at least three key sources: home, school, and media. He does acknowledge roles of "peers and related developmental factors" (page 29), but focuses on where he saw the most damage happening in the time his book was published at the end of the 20th century. (We'll consider some updates to his findings in just a bit.)

Shut-Down in the Home

Is the home environment for learning positively stimulating or is it otherwise? Numerous studies point to a child's first three years as crucial. Dr. Armstrong overviews four factors that can have an overall negative impact through disrupting development of the 12 Genius Qualities:

1. **Emotional dysfunction** (e.g., emotional problems, addictions). Such homes typically stunt learning with dynamics of control, perfectionism, and blaming. The family systems block children's freedom to think for themselves.

2. **Poverty**, since tasks related to survival cause emotional stress. Also, there are usually fewer activities and interactions that help children thrive and less stimulating in-home learning.

3. **A fast-paced lifestyle** where the family has the financial means to stimulate learning experiences, but there is pressure to do too much too soon. A competitive spirit is also common in these environments. This lifestyle can lead to children and teens giving up or burning out.

4. **Rigid ideologies** limit exposure to or exploration of other possibilities. It's difficult to develop open-mindedness in a closed system. This can happen in any philosophy, faith, or political view – left or right.

Shut-Down in School

New York University communication professor Neil Postman once wrote: "Children enter school as question marks and they leave school as periods." What happens in the interim?

For many children who have had their genius suppressed during the first five years of home life, school may simply add insult to injury and even further repress their genius qualities (page 34).

Dr. Armstrong is highly concerned about school environments that quench the genius qualities. Many school systems and teachers offer positive learning experiences, but many other elements can crush the joy of learning. Here are four of the worst offenders, according to Dr. Armstrong:

1. **Testing and grading** block the freedom to learn by dictating content, pace, and products. The judgment that typically comes with tests (and, in smaller doses, grading) brings stress and anxiety that cripple creativity.

2. **Labeling and tracking** emphasize "dissing" through such negative terms as <u>dis</u>abilities, <u>dis</u>order, and <u>dys</u>function – what students *can't* do instead of what they *can*. He notes that research suggests even those labeled as learning disabled or ADHD still have positive learning attributes. He also says that tracking classes (e.g., for "low-ability" students) have similar demotivating effects.

3. **Textbooks and Worksheet Learning.** "Most textbooks ought to be regarded as 'genius-unfriendly' because they generally convey the message that knowledge is 'information to be mastered,' not mysteries to be plumbed or exciting terrain to explore" (page 38).

4. **Tedium** deadens the mood for meaningful learning. "When tedium rules in a classroom, students divert their attention from the lesson plan and take their curiosity inside ('I wonder what Julie will be wearing to the dance this weekend?')" (page 40).

Shut-Down in the Media

"[B]ecause most television programming, computer games, and Internet fare are not being created by geniuses to awaken curiosity, wonder, or wisdom … our student's inborn genius is likely to find little nourishment from such influence" (page 41). There are four factors Dr. Armstrong mentions as the downfalls of these digital media:

1. **Violence.** The harm from violence in media was so apparent from research even in 1998 that he did not even elaborate on it, other than simply cite three studies.

2. **Stereotypical Images.** When ready-made images and preprogrammed storylines leave little to a child's imagination, life's realities get reduced to clichés. Instead of creativity or playfulness, what passes as "play" is actually passive consumption instead of active imagination.

3. **Insipid Language.** Interaction through language with adults has high impact on a child's development in its years. Where that growth could continue later on, media has instead substituted a flattened communication version that Library of America executive director Geoffrey O'Brien suggests "lacks figurative language, rhetorical complexity, eloquence, word-play, or historical or literary allusion" (page 43).

4. **Mediocre Content.** Infotainment may show elements of being creative, but that does not mean it inspires creativity in others. We're still inundated by junk information and media that detract, not enrich – and live in a world where (often uncivil) pop culture celebrities dominate over any who provoke growth through genius-quality thought, word, and deed.

Dr. Armstrong was highly aware of how discouraging this picture could look. However, he reminds teachers and the rest of us that:

> [E]ven in the most troubled and troublesome of learners the genius is still alive – somewhere. It may be buried under loads of put-downs, negative evaluations, low grades and test scores, delinquent behavior, self-hatred, and more, but like the seed in winter that lies dormant while braving the toughest storms and coldest arctic spells only to blossom with the sun's warmth in the spring, this genius too can survive if you will take the time to study the optimum conditions for its growth in the classroom. (page 48)

Bringing It All Up to Date

Dr. Armstrong wrote in 1998 about what awakens or stifles genius qualities in American culture. There's been immense upheaval in our world since then. So, it's natural to ask how seemingly irreversible changes in home, schools, and media/technology affect development of these 12 Genius Qualities. That is a huge subject, but it seems America is still on the same trajectory, but even accelerating toward increasing cultural shut-down of genius qualities in kids. Here are a few key thoughts on trends that make shut-down even more likely in certain domains now.

- **In the home** ... The past two decades have seen the economic gap widen between the haves and the have-nots, and home-life stability decrease from increases in patterns of family fragmentation and of relocation. These spotlight cultural differences that have more negative impact on children, in terms of their earliest development especially.

- **In the schools** ... There continues to be a mixture of freedom and restrictions, but an even stronger emphasis on standardized test-taking still pressures teachers and parents to teach toward tests instead of develop genius qualities for life.

- **In media and technology** ... Perhaps the starkest changes have been in ever-increasing consumption of media and technology. In 1998, the first wave of digital generations had not yet graduated from high school. Now those Millennials are in their early 30s, reared on almost constant access to technology. Yes, they can manipulate data fluidly. But mega-digital input appears to dampen more than enhance genius. For instance:

- ***Inventiveness*** requires use of simple raw materials, not merely the preprocessed products of someone else's electronic creativity.
- Though "information access" has increased, not all information is factual, and knowledge has never been the same as ***wisdom***.
- Virtual involvement is not the same as real-life exploration. Separation and isolation are in the "DNA" of many digital products, so the increase in sensory input they provide to us can still downplay ***sensitivity*** to the natural world around us.

What significant changes have you noticed, from the time you were children and adolescents until now, that seem to be stifling people's genius? Also, what might actually be giving them greater opportunities to awaken? The realities of the social changes and education in a digital era are not all bad and damaging. But they do require understanding. We strive to keep up with these topics at Celebrate Kids, Inc., because they strongly affect the core of children's developing security, identity, belonging, purpose, and competence – as well as their intelligences and genius. Our website has more resources to help you navigate teaching, parenting, and mentoring in the world as it now is.

Meanwhile, we'll end this section as with the earlier chapter on "How Genius Qualities Get Awakened" and its Awakening Words list. The following list of descriptive "Shut-Down Terms" was compiled from Dr. Armstrong's book, and the essays by both Dr. Kathy and Tina.

Shut-Down Terms

Admonish	Efficiency	React
Apathy	Fearful	Redefine
Atrophy	Force	Repress
Avoid	Guarded	Routine
Bland	Ignore	Rules
Lunt	Immobile	Ruts
Boredom	Insult	Self-protect
Brainwash	Isolate	Shame
Bury	Languish	Shortchange
Business as usual	Locked in	Shush
Commands	Managed	Snuff out
Compare	Misuse	Squeeze
Compel	Over Assume	Squealch
Contain	Overlook	Steal
Control	Overprotect	Stifle

Cover	Overtired	Stop
Cripple	Overwrought	Stymie
Crush	Paralyze	Subdue
Damage	Perfectionism	Suffocate
Deny	Placate	Survive
Depress	Preoccupied	Take for granted
Deconstructive	Pretense	Trigger
Disappoint	Procedure	Undervalue
Discount	Punish	
Disengage	Put-downs	
Don't apply		

[18]

Questions and Activities

Reflection Questions

Stifled genius qualities can be reawakened. How do you think that might happen? Is there any difference between that process and how they are usually awakened? What additional aspects might be needed to deal with them having been dampened in the first place?

Rigid, close-minded thinking diminishes the worth of these qualities. Do you listen to your children even when they ask questions about issues you're firm on?

Specifically in **school**, too much testing, grading, tedium, labeling, and tracking goes against these qualities. Do your children complain about these things? How can you help them not just cope with the tedium, but increasingly find other ways or activities on their own to counteract stifling and develop the qualities instead?

Being exposed to too much **mediocre media content** and its stereotypical images and insipid language makes it less likely that genius qualities will develop. How are the children and teens in your life doing, when it comes to media consumption? What do you think might be an appropriate level of TV-watching, game-playing, friend-texting, etc., and why? If you lead the way in decreasing media interaction, what might you replace that time with?

Emotional difficulties and dysfunction makes these qualities less likely. Stress, depression, fear, and the like in us and/or our kids steal the freedom necessary for these attributes to be exhibited. How emotionally healthy is your family? Regardless of its current state of health, what could you do to improve the quality of an emotionally stable environment, and growth in the genius qualities in the home?

Fast-track lifestyles allow little time for the off-the-book genius qualities. Would slowing down be good for you and your kids? If so, what activities might be good ones to start with, in terms of either removal or replacement with ones that are slower-paced?

Hints on Activities that Awaken Genius

Clustering the Qualities. One of Dr. Armstrong's biggest concerns for Multiple Intelligences and for the 12 Genius Qualities is that people would segment them from one another and over-focus on developing each one individually instead of integrating them. So, while some activities may emphasize a particular quality, keep in mind that it's more than okay to explore them for other qualities they can call forth. How could this or that experience serve as a "hub" for multiple aspects of intelligence and also for multiple genius qualities?

Externalizing and Role-Modeling. "Externalizing" is when we talk through the *process* of how we thought through a problem and came to a conclusion. It is the opposite of just telling someone our conclusion or opinion that was the product of our thinking. This role-models how to think. How might you apply this idea to developing genius qualities in the children and teens you influence? What are some genius qualities you feel most comfortable with, and what specific encounter or challenge or experience could you best use to externalize how it affected you? How about taking that same question, only this time identify a quality you are not so familiar with, trying to externalize while you plunge into it as something new (and perhaps a bit fearful!) to try as a growing experience you can do with your kids.

Variety in Activities. Many things have changed in our world since Dr. Armstrong published **Awakening Genius in the Classroom** in 1998 – some for better, some for worse. But a variety of activities will always be appropriate for individuals, families, and groups. To prepare the way, maybe you'd like to make a list of potential learning/exploring opportunities that fit with your locale. Here are some categories to consider, and some starter ideas:

- **Outdoor activities.** Kites in the park. Nature walk. Visit a farm or dairy. Plant an urban garden. Explore a vacant lot. Go to a different eco-system. Miniature golf.
- **Indoor activities.** Board games. Imaginative play. Experiments. Rearrange furniture/redesign rooms.

Clean out the garage and discover what's there. Bowling. Cooking.

- **Field trips.** Art exhibit. Aquarium. Museum. Unusual buildings on the local historical register. Urban scavenger hunt or geocaching trip.
- **General possibilities.** Technology-free day. Interact with and talk about technology. Family time. Read together and discuss reactions. Volunteer together.

Digital Dilemmas. Technology may make certain data and experiences much more accessible, but not necessarily more developmental, in terms of the 12 Genius Qualities. What kinds of electronics and media could help amplify the exploration of genius qualities, and how? What kinds seem more probable to cause them to shut down? What sorts of changes in your and your children's usages of media and digital gadgets might be beneficial for (re)awakening genius?

Genius Quality Conversations. As we go about our day with the children and teens we influence, it's important to listen carefully and engage in meaningful conversations. You may find it helpful to understand them better by getting more background on Multiple Intelligences, to see what kinds of activities might best spark the 12 Genius Qualities for specific children. That may provide a far easier bridge to deeper interactions about what they find to be passionate about in particular activities that intrigue them. And don't forget questions that help them draw out their thought processes and feelings: What do you think? What else could that be? How does that make you feel? What do you most like about this? Show me what you mean.

Compliment Specifically. As Dr. Kathy teaches in her booklet, *Complimenting and Correcting, The Power of Doing it Well*, and on her CD, *Fabulous Feedback*, the use of specific language helps children continue the good we want to see more of. Therefore, when we see our children using one of these genius qualities, rather than telling them they were "good" or "clever" let's remember to observe carefully so we can tell them which quality they used. Were they curious, playful, imaginative, creative, wondering, using wisdom, inventive, vital, sensitive, flexible, humorous, or joyful?

Develop Character and Other-Centeredness. For children to use these qualities in healthy ways so they don't get into trouble, they must be encouraged to respect themselves and others and be self-controlled. They must be taught these heart-based qualities. They also must learn to consider others to make sure their uses of these qualities don't put others at risk or cause stress.

12 Genius Qualities Chapter Quotes

1. Curiosity: "To ask questions that others judge as irrelevant." (p. 3)
2. Playfulness: "An attitude toward life." (p. 5)
3. Imagination: "To close their eyes and 'see' ..." (p. 5)
4. Creativity: "To give birth to new ways of looking at things." (p. 6)
5. Wonder: "Natural astonishment about the world." (p. 7)
6. Wisdom: "[T]o experience the wonder of the world directly, without the blinders of preconceptions and clichés." (p. 8)
7. Inventiveness: "A 'hands-on' creativity; creating new things from known things." (p. 9)
8. Vitality: "Being awake to your senses, totally and immediately responsive to the environment, and actively engaged in each and every moment." (p. 10)
9. Sensitivity: "The incredible openness that children have to the world." (p. 11)
10. Flexibility: "The ability of children to make fluid associations." (p. 12)
11. Humor: "Looking at things differently; a trait that breaks us out of ruts and routines and causes 'aliveness' to occur." (p.13)

12. Joy: "Comes from deep inside us when a new connection is made, a new insight obtained, a new feat accomplished, or a skill mastered." (p. 14)

These definitions are taken from Dr. Thomas Armstrong's book *Awakening Genius in the Classroom*.

References and Resources

Awakening Genius in the Classroom, by Thomas Armstrong (Association for Supervision and Curriculum Development, 1998).

Finding Authentic Hope and Wholeness: 5 Questions That Will Change Your Life, by Kathy Koch (Moody Publishers, 2005).

Frames of Mind: The Theory of Multiple Intelligences, by Howard Gardner (Basic Books, 1983). This classic work is now in its Third Edition, published in 2011.

8 Great Smarts Discover and Nurture Your Child's Intelligences, by Kathy Koch (Moody Publishers, 2016).

The Read-Aloud Handbook, by Jim Trelease (Penguin Books, Seventh Edition, 2013).

Read for Your Life: Turning Teens into Readers, by Gladys Hunt and Barbara Hampton (Zondervan, Annotated Edition, 1992).

7 Kinds of Smart: Identifying and Developing Your Multiple Intelligences, by Thomas Armstrong (Plume, Revised Updated Edition, 1999).

Photo Licensing/Copyright Information

The following photographs were licensed by Celebrate Kids, Inc., from **Fotolia.com**.

How Genius Qualities Get Awakened

- **Coaches and Trainers.** #19538875 - Young Boys And Girls In Football Team With Coach - © Monkey Business / Fotolia.
- **Teachers and Mentors.** #2844269 – councelling © Arvind Balaraman / Fotolia.
- **Parents and Community Members.** #37352609 - Father and daughter with a fishing net © auremar / Fotolia.

12 Genius Qualities

- **#1 Curiosity.** #27922753 - Boy With Down syndrome Singing into Microphone © Gino Santa Maria / Fotolia.
- **#2 Playfulness.** #25404895 - enfant jouant © RomainQuéré / Fotolia.

- **#3 Imagination**. #47709689 - Asian family reading book © WONG SZE FEI / Fotolia.
- **#4 Creativity**. #39624041 - Young boy making gingerbread men © bst2012 / Fotolia.
- **#5 Wonder**. #39635416 - Young girl looking at baby seal on rocks © bst2012 / Fotolia.
- **#6 Wisdom**. #25524396 - Fillette présentant une maison à énergie positive. © Prod. Numérik / Fotolia.
- **#7 Inventiveness**. #41216498 - Child hobby © jeecis / Fotolia.
- **#8 Vitality**. #57738741 - Happy boy with autumn leaves © Iosif Szasz-Fabian / Fotolia.
- **#9 Sensitivity**. #41632851 - Comforting little girl © auremar / Fotolia.
- **#10 Flexibility**. #46495864 - Science Education School Boy Writing © HaywireMedia / Fotolia.
- **#11 Humor**. #28899793 - Boy Blowing Huge Bubble With Bubble Gum © Vibe Images / Fotolia.
- **#12 Joy**. #45787249 - Elementary pupils in classroom during lesson © Petro Feketa / Fotolia.

How Genius Qualities Get Shut Down
- **Factors at Home**. #55312689 - 親子ケンカ["Parent-child fights"] © hinata815 / Fotolia.

- **Factors at School.** #11943055 – Child © metrmetr / Fotolia.
- **Factors in Media.** #942094 - business boy 19 © Paul Moore / Fotolia.

Whether this is your first connection with **Celebrate Kids, Inc.**, or you've been introduced to our work already, we're glad you're here – and welcome! Our purpose is to inspire, encourage, and equip you to become better as a parent, educator, and/or mentor to the children and teenagers in your life. To help you influence the kids you're connected with, we've produced materials on a variety of relevant topics, including people's core needs, learning styles, and personal growth.

Celebrate Kids, Inc.
www.celebratekids.com
www.DrKathyKoch.com
www.facebook.com/celebratekidsinc
vimeo.com/channels/Kathyisms
www.instagram.com/kathycelebrate
www.pinterest.com/kathycelebrate

ABOUT THE AUTHORS

Dr. Kathy Koch ("cook") is the Founder and President of Celebrate Kids, Inc., based in Fort Worth, TX. Her love for Jesus and her faith and desire to serve and glorify God are the foundations of her ministry. A Chatty Kathy as a child, she now speaks to parents, educators, pastors, students of all ages, and missionaries nationally and internationally.

Kathy shares keynote messages, seminars, assemblies, and chapels in schools, churches, and convention settings. She's been privileged to do that in over 25 countries since 1991. She also blogs regularly and enjoys influencing and connecting with people on other social media platforms. She and her staff also create products that support her main messages.

Dr. Kathy is an author for Moody Publishing. With Jill Savage, she wrote *No More Perfect Kids: Love Your Kids For Who They Are*. The truths help parents understand why they must get to know their children to parent them according to their design. *8 Great Smarts Discover and Nurture Your Child's Intelligences* helps parents and teachers better understand children's learning strengths. *Finding Authentic Hope and Wholeness: 5 Questions That Will Change Your Life* provides a solution-focused, enriching approach to real problems. In March, 2015, her book **Screens and Teens: Connecting with Our Kids in a Wireless World** was published.

Before moving to Fort Worth to establish her ministry, Kathy served as a tenured Associate Professor in the education department at the University of Wisconsin-Green Bay. She also taught second grade, coached at the middle school level, and served as a school board member for a Christian school. Kathy earned three degrees from Purdue University, including a Ph.D. in reading and educational psychology.

Tina Hollenbeck is the creator and coordinator of The Homeschool Resource Roadmap, a database of over 2,000 curricula and support materials for homeschooling families classified by common core status, subject area, and worldview. Through this initiative, she seeks to provide useful information and encouragement so that those called to educate and disciple their own children will be confident and equipped for the task.

Tina lives in Green Bay, WI. She and her husband Jeff are the parents of three precious daughters, one of whom is already in heaven with Christ. She taught in the public schools prior to having her children and choosing to educate them at home. She enjoys serving on her church's worship team and exercising, even at 5:30 a.m.!

Dr. Kathy met Tina when she was Kathy's student at the University of Wisconsin-Green Bay. She recognized Tina's talent as a thinker, writer, and educator, so inviting her to be a staff writer with Celebrate Kids was an easy decision. She's done that since 2006 and occasionally speaks on our behalf, as well.

Brad Sargent is based near San Francisco and is a cultural interpreter, futurist, and organizational developer. He gets great satisfaction from helping others identify, validate, amplify, and activate their unique strengths and purposes. He enjoys networking people and causes together for the good of Christ's Kingdom.

Brad has been volunteering and working in community, media, and ministry roles since 1972. He uses those experiences to do research writing on healthy versus toxic organizations and to design strategies for creating safe work/ministry environments. He is also co-creator with Shannon Hopkins and Andy Schofield of *The Transformation Index*. It is a set of project planning tools people can use to identify desired social changes; design, implement, and evaluate plans; and measure the impact of change both qualitatively and quantitatively.

Brad's current project is *Do Good Plus Do No Harm*, a systems guidebook on paradigm shifts and social transformation for social enterprises and faith-based missional ministries. He enjoys writing a cappella songs and performing, the mystery and majesty of cultures of the world, and finding movies that highlight the many things he finds intriguing about the process of personal and social change.

Brad and Dr. Kathy met in the mid-1990s and have partnered on several projects since then. Most significantly, he was her project manager on her first book. He is a definite thought leader and has helped her with significant research, editing, and writing.